Thrills o

Written by Brylee Gibson

PEARSON

Thrills on Water!

Water sports can be thrilling but dangerous. People who like to do water sports must learn them well.

There are many different ways to do water sports and different things to use. People can use boats, boards, kites and even fins.

kitesurfing

surfing

kayaking

Surfing can be a thrilling but dangerous sport. Some surfers like to surf giant waves. These waves are so big that sometimes the surfers can't paddle fast enough to catch them. The surfers can be towed into the wave by a jet ski.

When the jet ski gets to the top of the wave, the surfer lets go of the rope and surfs down the wave. The surfer will be going very fast.

Jaws Hawaii

surfer
jet ski

Put your feet in here.
foot straps
kiteboard

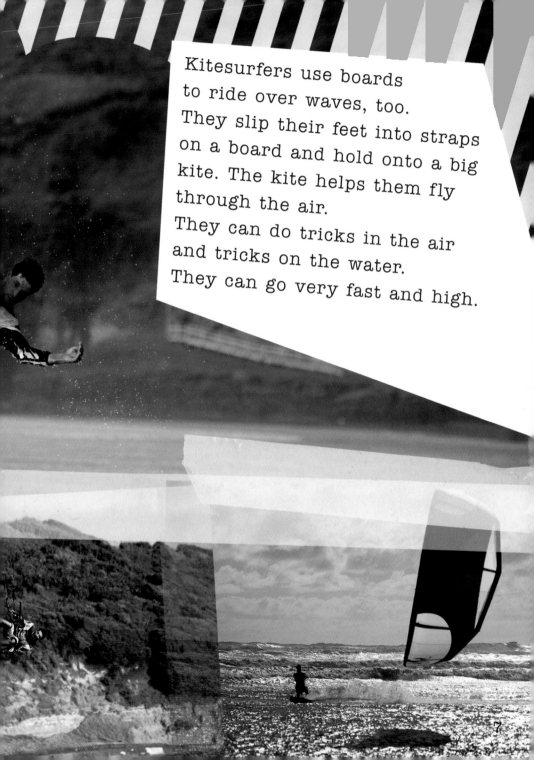

Kitesurfers use boards
to ride over waves, too.
They slip their feet into straps
on a board and hold onto a big
kite. The kite helps them fly
through the air.
They can do tricks in the air
and tricks on the water.
They can go very fast and high.

. . . backwards

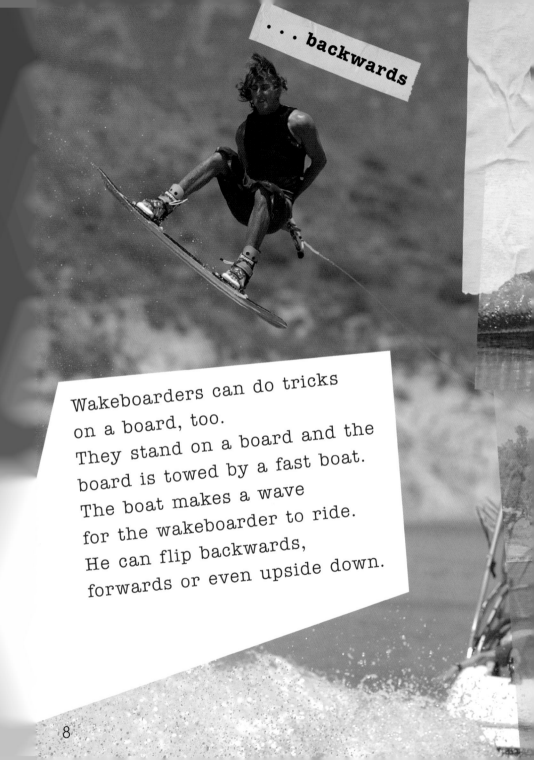

Wakeboarders can do tricks
on a board, too.
They stand on a board and the
board is towed by a fast boat.
The boat makes a wave
for the wakeboarder to ride.
He can flip backwards,
forwards or even upside down.

. . . upside down

This person is towed behind a fast boat, too. But there is no board for him to stand on. He stands on his bare feet! He is a barefoot skier.

The boat must go very fast for a barefoot skier to stand up.

Barefoot skiers must curl their toes up so that they don't dig into the water. If they dig their toes into the water, they will fall over.

Some people like to go down rivers in a rubber raft. The river can be dangerous. The water can move very fast and there can be hidden rocks. The rubber raft can bounce off the rocks. The people have to hang on tight and steer the raft carefully with their paddles.

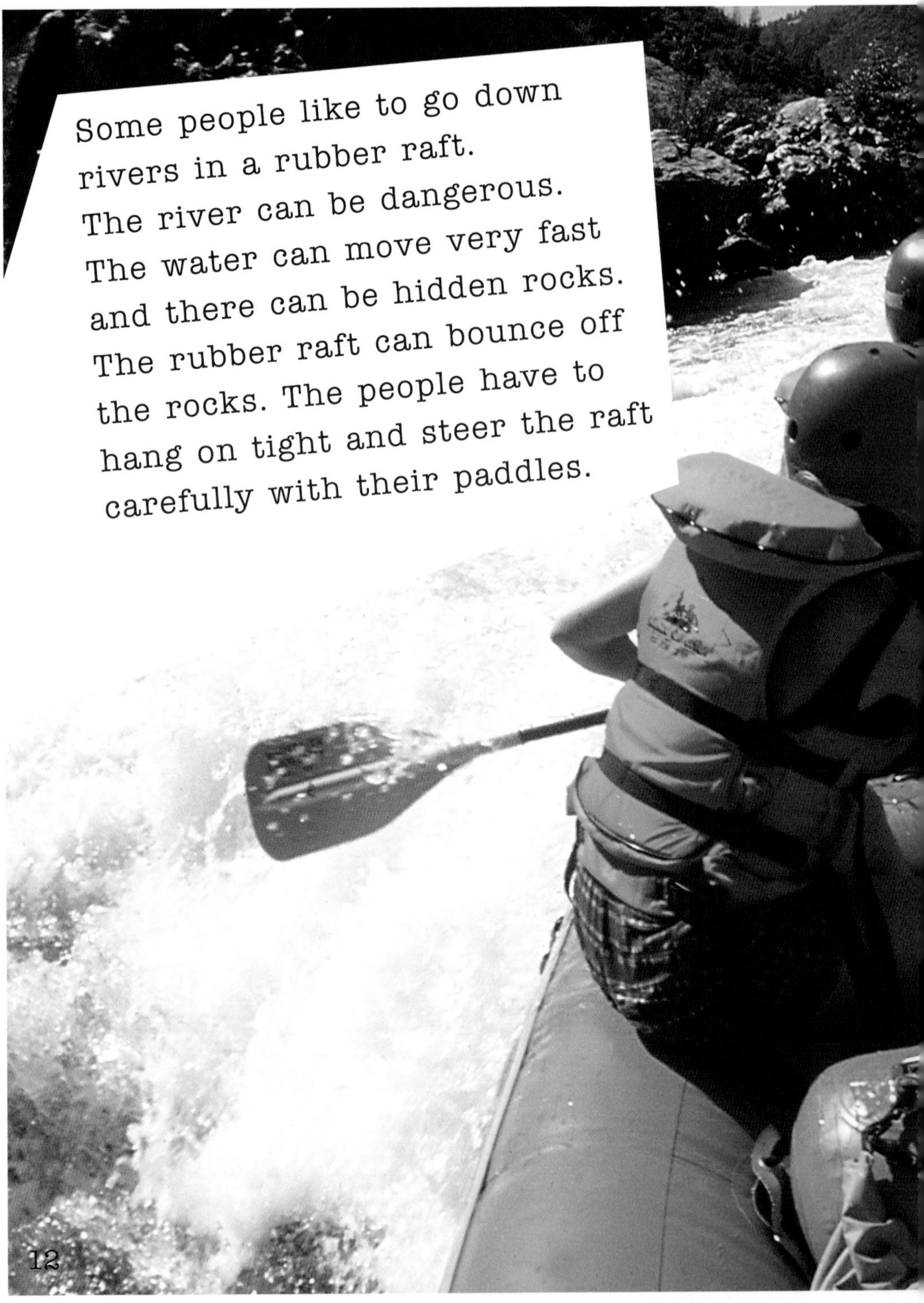

Some people like to go down rivers and over waterfalls in a kayak. The water can be going so fast, their kayak can flip over. But the people won't fall out, because they wear a spray skirt. The skirt fits onto the kayak and helps to keep them safely inside. If a person flips upside down, they can pull a strap on the skirt to get out of the kayak.

spray skirt
Pull the strap
to undo the skirt.
The skirt fits here.

These people are called free divers.
Their sport is not **on** the water,
but **under** the water.
Free divers hold their breath and
dive down into the water.
They like to see how deep they can go.
Some divers wear a big fin,
like a fish's tail.
The fin helps them move quickly.

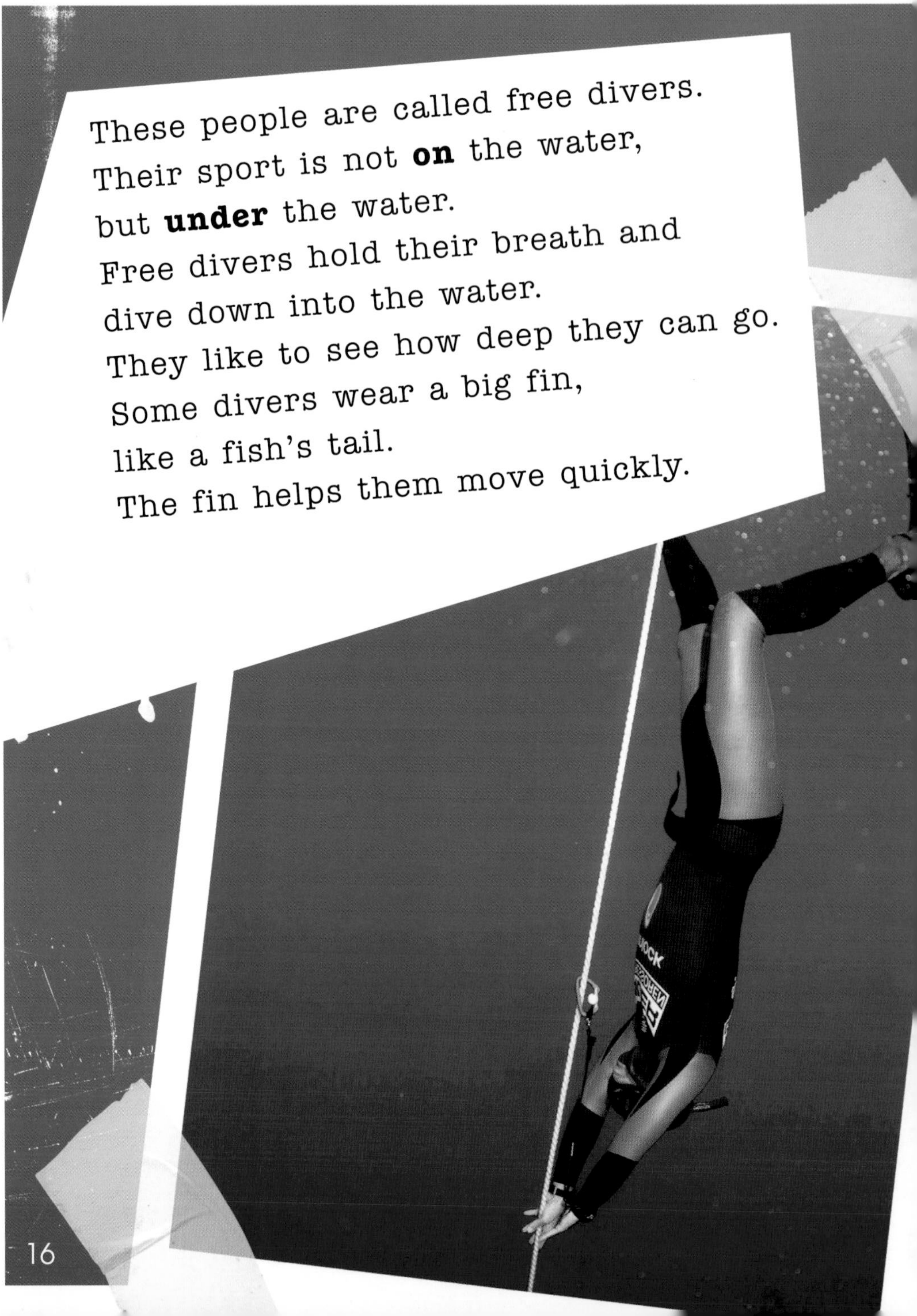

Some free divers can dive up to 90m deep.

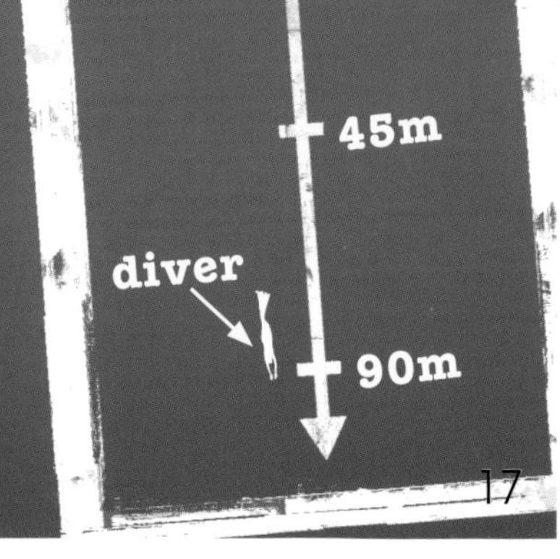

surfing

kitesurfing

ee diving

Thrills on Water!

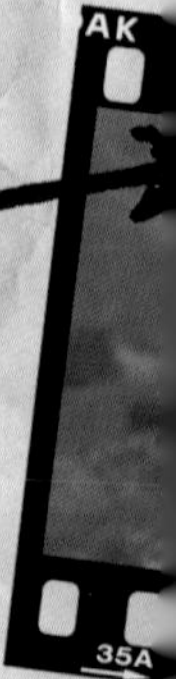

barefoot skiing

kayaking

white-water rafting

wakeboarding

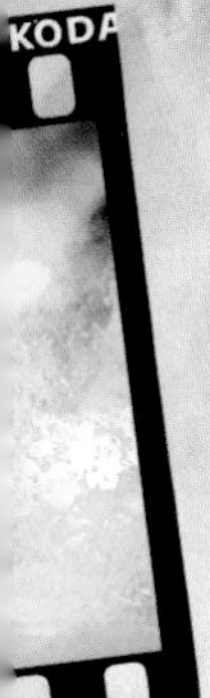

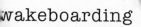

Index

Guide Notes

Title: Thrills on Water!

Stage: Launching Fluency – Orange

Genre: Non-fiction

Approach: Guided Reading

Processes: Thinking Critically, Exploring Language, Processing Information

Written and Visual Focus: Graph, Labels, Captions, Index

Word Count: 449

Thinking Critically

(sample questions)

- What do you think is meant by *thrills on water*? What do you know about thrills people might have on or in water?
- What might you expect to see in this book?
- Look at the index. Encourage the students to think about the information and make predictions about the text content.
- Look at pages 4 and 5. Why do you think surfing could be a dangerous sport?
- Look at pages 6 and 7. Why do you think the kitesurfer's feet need to be strapped onto the board?
- Look at pages 8 and 9. Why do you think the wakeboarder needs a fast boat?
- Look at pages 10 and 11. Do you think barefoot skiing would be thrilling? Why do you think that?
- Look at pages 12 and 13. Why do you think the raft might be made of rubber?
- What things in the book have helped you to understand the information?
- What questions do you have after reading the text?

Exploring Language

Terminology

Photograph credits, index

Vocabulary

Clarify: straps, towed, kayak, steer

Singular/Plural: sport/sports, wave/waves, toe/toes

Homonyms: tow/toe, too/two/to, board/bored

Print Conventions

Apostrophes – possessives (fish's), contractions (can't, don't, won't)